COOL CAREERS WITHOUT COLLEGE
FOR PEOPLE WHO LOVE

PLANNING AND
ORGANIZING

REBECCA PELOS AND ROBERT GREENBERGER

Rosen
YA
New York

In memory of 32 Summerhill, home of M, H, M, A, and J

Published in 2018 by The Rosen Publishing Group, Inc.
29 East 21st Street, New York, NY 10010

Copyright © 2018 by The Rosen Publishing Group, Inc.

First Edition

Library of Congress Cataloging-in-Publication Data

Names: Pelos, Rebecca, author. | Greenberger, Robert, author.
Title: Cool careers without college for people who love planning and organizing / Rebecca Pelos and Robert Greenberger.
Description: First edition. | New York, NY : Rosen Publishing, [2018] | Series: Cool careers without college | Includes bibliographical references and index.
Identifiers: LCCN 2016053661 | ISBN 9781508175407 (library bound)
Subjects: LCSH: Management—Vocational guidance—Juvenile literature. | Occupations—Juvenile literature
Classification: LCC HD38.2 .P45 2017 | DDC 331.702—dc23
LC record available at https://lccn.loc.gov/2016053661

Manufactured in the United States of America

CONTENTS

INTRODUCTION

Y ou're the type of person who color codes your homework folders. You don't plan a *thing* without checking your phone for scheduling conflicts. If someone tells you that you're in charge of planning a friend's party, you know that that party will be a guaranteed success. You're a "planner." You love being organized. And the good news is that there's a career in that. You might not even have to budget for college in order to make it happen.

If you love to plan and organize, there are a lot of career fields that offer opportunities that align with your interests. You can use your skills to professionally organize another person's life, coordinate travel plans for a busy executive, help raise funds for worthy causes…the possibilities are endless! And for many of these career paths, you can sidestep going to college, which has become a pretty popular choice among a lot of today's high school graduates. It's more affordable, doesn't saddle students with future debt, and allows for flexibility if you decide to change careers down the road.

In the following sections, you will get to explore thirteen different avenues toward a career where you can utilize your organizing talents and flourish in a tough, competitive job market. The time is now…to get organized!

Being organized is helpful in school and whatever career path you choose, so it's good to develop excellent habits now. Keeping a planner is a great place to start.

CHAPTER 1

WEDDING COORDINATOR/ PARTY PLANNER

Parties celebrate holidays, work events, weddings, birthdays, pretty much anything that a party enthusiast's heart desires. And when the situation calls for everything to go off without a hitch, that often calls for a party planner to take charge. The role of the event or party planner, a job title that didn't formally exist before 1990, has evolved over the past decade into one of the fastest-growing fields in the United States. Party planning entails everything from corporate functions to personal parties. With so many choices, more and more people bring in a professional to help bring their dream event to life.

WHAT THEY DO

Party and wedding planners are usually small businesses with a large network of outside resources and contacts. A deep knowledge of local venues and vendors is essential to make an event successful. Some companies have their own staff to handle assignments, but most bring in outside experts.

Wedding planners work one-on-one with the bride and groom to help bring their vision to life.

Party planners must be experts in a wide variety of areas. They need to know where to hire entertainers and musicians, where to buy the right kind of food and flowers, and how best to let people know where and when the event is occurring.

About.com describes the skills required for a wedding planner, skills that apply to most other events as well: "A wedding planner must be able to remain calm in the face of adversity. Of course, he or she must be personable and, … [be] a good negotiator. You are the mouthpiece for the bride and groom when it comes to ordering flowers, hiring a band and photographer, finding a caterer, [and more]. You must be able to get them the best service for the lowest price—your reputation will depend on it. Networking is also important. Establishing good connections will help ensure that you get good deals. That's not all. Running your own business, as well as handling someone else's money, requires that you be adept at handling finances. You must also be very well organized."

PLANNING YOUR CAREER

Wedding or party planners must have a very strong design sense and a way with fashion. He or she should know about color, music, and flowers. A good knowledge of religions is also important since wedding ceremonies are also often religious. Party planners and wedding planners in particular should have detailed knowledge of many

KOOL EVENTS PARTY PLANNING

Kool Events is a New York City–based full-service planning service run by Anne Morin and Amy Kool. "I'm an artist, Anne's a musician," Kool says. "When I graduated in the 1980s, I found there were [too few] jobs for artists … I ended up working in the entertainment field." Kool and her partner worked at various nightclubs for more than a decade. As Wall Street firms and other corporations expanded their businesses, there was a need for planning corporate events.

"Companies wanted something different, fun things like theme parties, team-building events, networking, and client entertainment. I was involved with music, catering, entertainment, and coming up with ideas for different types of events.

"For us, it was great because we're creative people, my art background allowed me to look at a space and envision how it would look with the finished themes and party designs.

"One of my most favorite parties was for Ketchum Publishing. They were releasing a cookbook with recipes from markets of the world, so we turned the space into an international marketplace. People attending the author's book signing party got gold coins to purchase items at the booths."

"A client calls," Kool says of a typical event, "and we first get specifications including time, concept, budget, and the number of people involved. We then find a location, plan a menu or work with the restaurant/venue, plan the event's schedule, and determine if there are giveaways [or favors]."

Once the client likes the proposal from Kool Events, they sign a contract and then the staff gets to work. Since they do not advertise, they rely entirely on referrals. After months of planning,

(continued on the next page)

(continued from the previous page)

Kool or her staff will arrive on-site. Did the right food, flowers, decorations, and audio/visual equipment arrive on time? Is everything provided as planned?

Summing up, Kool identifies the traits a person needs to succeed in this field: "To do events [well] you need imagination, a knowledge of wines and foods; an understanding of how furniture fits into space, how to make things flow; you have to be a perfectionist. You have to be flexible since there's always a problem to handle. You have to be patient; you're dealing with human beings. You need good communication and writing skills. You have to be able to write down descriptions of events in a clear way; you have to be able to correspond with people; you have to have some command of the English language. You can't write a terrible proposal, it has to be literate."

different types of cultural ceremonies. Keeping up with the latest trends is also vital.

Although college degrees are not required to be a party or wedding planner, basic business skills are always useful. Relevant courses in high school include economics, marketing, creative writing, math, English, and art. Once you decide to start your own planning business, iVillage.com estimates the following start-up costs: $2,000 and up for a computer and software; $100 to $5,000 to market yourself via advertisements in the yellow pages, other local publications, and through direct-mail campaigns; and $500 and up for your wardrobe. The vast majority of planners work from home offices, so rent is not a major issue.

Just about everything that is normally needed for a wedding can be applied to parties that may range from a sweet-sixteen dance to a retirement function. Again, the planner tailors the event to the desires of its guest of honor and his or her friends and family, finding the best possible location, overall theme, menu, cake, decorations, and so on, down to the smallest details. The latest trend among event planners, according to a July 2005 *USA Today* article, is planning customized funerals. One noteworthy example was that of a passionate football fan who was embalmed, propped in his favorite recliner, and situated as if he were about to watch the weekend games.

Several consultants suggest volunteering with an established planner as a valuable way to evaluate how suited you are

Wedding planners must keep track of every detail: decorations, ensuring you have the a water glass for each guest, or making sure that the caterer can find a parking spot close to the venue.

to the business and to make important contacts at the same time. Given the popularity of the field, some small companies receive upward of fifty résumés a week from people looking to get started. People who work for these firms usually start with minimum wage and work their way up based on their efficiency, communication, and social skills.

JOB OUTLOOK AND SALARY

The fees that party and wedding planners charged is constantly changing and can be adjusted as necessary. Typically, planners charge a fee of 10 to 15 percent of the cost of an event to organize and manage it. This means that your annual salary will vary greatly depending upon the amount of work you do, where you live, and how successful you are at planning events.

Party and wedding planning is a new field, so available data is scant. However, jobs such as these are becoming more widespread. More and more individuals seem to be tapping into the skills of successful planners, not just brides and up-and-coming corporate types.

FOR MORE INFORMATION

ORGANIZATIONS

Association of Bridal Consultants
56 Danbury Road, Suite 11
New Milford, CT 06776
(860) 355-7000
Website: http://www.bridalassn.com
This organization of reputable wedding planners and
professionals holds members to high standards,
guaranteeing a job well done.

International Live Events Association
330 N Wabash Ave
Chicago, IL 60611
(800) 688-4737
Website: http://www.ileahub.com
This association represents and supports a membership
of more than five thousand live event professionals
who do business together, share knowledge, nurture
talent, and grow their industry.

National Association of Catering Executives (NACE)
10440 Little Patuxent Parkway, Suite 300
Columbia, MD 21044
(410) 290-5410

Website: http://nace.net
NACE works to raise the standard of professionalism in the catering industry through education, certification, standards, ethics, and professional recognition programs.

BOOKS

Roney, Carley. *The Knot Ultimate Wedding Planner & Organizer: Worksheets, Checklists, Etiquette, Calendars, and Answers to Frequently Asked Questions.* New York, NY: Random House, 2013.

Touchstone, Gemma. *Party Style: Kids' Parties from Baby to Sweet 16.* Springville, UT: Cedar Fort, 2015.

WEBSITES

Because of the changing nature of internet links, Rosen Publishing has developed an online list of websites related to the subject of this book. This site is updated regularly. Please use this link to access the list:

http://www.rosenlinks.com/CCWC/planning

CHAPTER 2

PROFESSIONAL LIFE COACH

Looking at your own life, seeing that there are issues, and trying to figure out how to solve them is a huge undertaking. Some people turn to a life coach for assistance. This is a person who makes a career out of offering a confused person a fresh, objective perspective and often a serious examination and assessment of his or her client's choices and future.

WHAT THEY DO

Life coaches listen to their clients, try to understand a multitude of obstacles and situations, and then begin to work on charting a course for that individual's self-fulfillment. They work with people in all walks of life, in different professions and circumstances. As a result, a life coach needs to understand not just the person and his or her personal circumstances, but the career to which he or she aspires. Unlike a professional organizer, a life coach works with concrete facts as well as spiritual and philosophical issues, so the word "coach" is entirely appropriate.

Life coaches advise clients on a variety of specific needs, including career advice and interpersonal relationships.

Coachlink.net describes the life coach profession as follows: "Coaching integrates principles from the fields of education, psychology, business, and personal transformation. Your coach serves as your personal consultant, partner, sounding board, and confidante, championing you to improve your effectiveness and achieve your goals. Your coach partners with you to improve your focus, to hold yourself accountable, and celebrate your successes."

In the best-case scenario, life coaches will help their clients develop their natural abilities and channel those into a rewarding career. Life coaching, however, is not therapy. If a client requires the assistance of a psychologist, psychotherapist, or psychiatrist, then he or she should seek that help immediately. Unlike close friends or associates, life coaches can objectively zero in on his or her client's career and job experience. A life coach outlines a person's good and bad points in a truthful way and teaches a client methods to accentuate the positive.

Businessballs.com, a reference source for corporate executives, notes, "[Life] coaching is a relatively new and different profession—different [from] psychology, counseling, or therapy. The big difference between coaching and these professions is that coaching doesn't claim to have the answers. A coach's job is not to go over old ground, be past-orientated, or to force-feed information, but to work with clients *to help them find the answers themselves.*"

Andrea Howard, an employment counselor with the New York State Department of Labor explains, "[Life] coaches help define goals and obtain excellence. The job search process can be tough on the self-esteem. Repeated rejections can be discouraging. Coaches offer support, motivation, and encouragement. Coaches listen to detect thoughts, feelings, and aspirations related to career decision-making. They also ask questions and provide feedback on clients' strengths,

Many life coaches can work from home, providing advice on the phone or through social media, but most prefer to meet with clients one-on-one.

insecurities, concerns, areas of need, and career-related obstacles. They help clients develop goals and achieve a higher level of performance and satisfaction."

The coaching process can occur in person or by phone, less often by email. Some arrangements blend all three, although coaches tend to prefer one method or another. A person seeking a life coach needs to make a commitment of time since a single session only identifies the problem. Normally, life coaches look for a three-month plan, some as many as six months.

Life coaches will tell you that they are not miracle workers, and the client must be willing to use the advice and implement it. A successful coach will provide a clear plan for achieving the identified goals, teach you skills to put the plan into action, and help find ways to keep you focused. If successful, the lessons taught by a coach can last a person the rest of his or her life.

PREPARING FOR YOUR CAREER

Life coaches impart many lessons while working with a client. Some of these lessons may appear to be common sense, but he or she has to find ways to communicate in terms the client will comprehend and accept. For would-be coaches, there are many private companies willing to teach you those methods for a price. The entire field is not regulated or tracked by the federal government, so standards vary from company to company.

There are two organizations that offer certification, each subscribing to a code of ethics and practices. There are many other organizations for life coaches in this still growing field. Most companies suggest that life coaches have experience in other fields, too, and bring those experiences to bear when helping others. Some organizations such as Coachlink, insist that their coaches have also been clients so they understand the other side of the process.

SALARY EXPECTATIONS

Life coaches can determine their own salary, based on experience, location, and number of clients. Once selected by a client, the coach then outlines the schedule of meetings, method of meeting, and an estimate for the duration of the relationship. From there an estimate of the fee structure is outlined and an agreement is usually made between coach and client.

The fee structure will vary. But generally, life coaches can earn well with just a few forty-five-minute sessions per day, either conducted in person or on the telephone. Subsequent sessions will vary depending upon the agreed-upon pricing structure.

FOR MORE INFORMATION

ORGANIZATIONS

International Association of Professional Life Coaches
1932 Gear Avenue #4
Fairfield, IA 52556
(641) 919-8910
Website: http://iaplifecoaches.org
This association inspires, promotes, and supports
life coaches around the world so they can coach
the people they were meant to serve and run a
profitable business.

International Coach Federation
2365 Harrodsburg Road, Suite A325
Lexington, KY 40504
(888) 423-3131
Website: http://www.coachfederation.org
This nonprofit organization allows fellow coaches to
support each other and grow the profession.

Worldwide Association of Business Coaches (WABC)
c/o WABC Coaches Inc.
Box 215
Saanichton, BC V8M 2C3
Canada

Website: http://www.wabccoaches.com
This Canadian-based association of professional
    business coaches allows for networking and business-
    building strategy.

BOOKS

Covey, Stephen R. *The Seven Habits of Highly Effective People, Anniversary Edition*. New York, NY: Simon & Schuster, 2013.
McLean, Pamela. *The Completely Revised Handbook of Coaching: A Developmental Approach*. Hoboken, NJ: Jossey-Bass, 2012.
Rydall, Derek. *Emergence: Seven Steps for Radical Life Change*. New York, NY: Atria Books, 2015.

WEBSITES

Because of the changing nature of internet links, Rosen Publishing has developed an online list of websites related to the subject of this book. This site is updated regularly. Please use this link to access the list:

http://www.rosenlinks.com/CCWC/planning

CHAPTER 3

PERSONAL AIDE/ ADMINISTRATIVE ASSISTANT

There will always be a need for clerks, secretaries, and administrative assistants. According to the United States Department of Labor statistics, there were around four million administrative jobs available in 2014. Careers as personal assistants are far reaching, with positions in many areas ranging from home health care to running what is essentially a small business.

WHAT THEY DO

Personal assistants are responsible for maintaining someone else's life: organizing, running errands, and making sure things large and small are accomplished in a timely fashion. Personal assistants have to remember many details, from a boss's spouse's birthday to bringing in the dry cleaning. In some cases, the personal assistant for a corporate officer will be expected to blur the line between professional obligations and personal ones. In just about every case, the hours for personal assistants are long.

An administrative assistant's tasks run the gamut from the ordinary (like making copies) to the exciting (like handling a meet and greet with a celebrity client). Every day is unique!

Depending upon the position, the personal assistant will be required to know basic computer software such as Microsoft Word, Excel, and Outlook. In these days of wireless technology, you are also likely to encounter a variety of hand-held devices too, such as cell phones and PDAs (personal digital assistants). For those caring for the ill, understanding IVs, catheters, pill schedules, and oxygen tanks are a set of skills required.

Of the jobs posted, the most glamorous might sound like the following: "A-list celebrity/actor seeks personal assistant live-out position with travel. Will support with all aspects of her personal life. Arrange family, personal, and business matters. Plan events for business and pleasure. Assist in maintaining households. Requires a flexible schedule for travel. Quick thinking, resourceful, and being able to switch gears is necessary."

Sounds exciting, right? But look more closely at the description. You will also be asked to do mundane household tasks as part of the job. Maintaining the house could mean time spent food shopping or even dusting. This description sounds a little less thrilling, right?

To qualify, the ad also states: "Three years minimum serving as a personal assistant, BA or equivalent experience, excellent communication skills, must have prior entertainment/production experience."

In the Princeton Review's *Best Entry-Level Jobs*, one celebrity personal assistant said, "I was too naïve at that point to know [that I should negotiate my starting salary]. It could've been negotiable, but it was so exciting to be offered the job that I didn't ask." Asked to name the fringe benefits of their job, assistants list "free travel and life experience" and "the opportunity to know an American legend on a personal basis." For a personal assistant to a major fashion designer, the major perk was "the clothes, hands down. We had the best wardrobes in town."

Positions available as personal assistants for celebrities are infrequent opportunities. Many more PA jobs come from the corporate world. An ad for a major clothing chain was looking for an executive administrative assistant who would be required to do the following:

- Manage executive calendar and schedule appointments
- Screen incoming calls and correspondence and respond independently when possible
- Arrange programs, events, or conferences by arranging for facilities and issuing information or invitations
- Direct preparation of records such as agendas, notices, minutes, and resolutions for department meetings
- Type correspondences to include letters, memos, forms, etc.
- Arrange complex and detailed travel plans and itineraries and compile documents for travel-related meetings
- Assist with preparation of departmental reports
- Coordinate recruitment process with HR and colleges for hiring assistant buyers
- Edit and process departmental timesheets for payroll purposes
- Order and keep inventory of supplies
- Coordinate all record keeping as required

It sounds like the description of a secretary; well, maybe more than a typical secretary, hence the word "executive" in the title. These days, calling someone a secretary might seem a little outdated, so the title has morphed into administrative assistant, personal assistant, and beyond. The duties, though, have not necessarily changed.

The requirements in this case include: "A seasoned administrative professional with at least three years of office management experience. Excellent verbal and written communication skills are paramount, as are solid organizational and multitasking skills. Computer proficiency in MS Office is an absolute must. This person must also be flexible to work overtime as needed and capable of handling time-sensitive and confidential information."

Why do executives or professionals or even actors need a personal assistant? *Realtor* magazine says, "Hiring a personal assistant can boost your production from mid-level performance to top-producing status. But your level of success depends on what you want the assistant to do—secretarial work or hands-on real estate support— whether the person is licensed or unlicensed, what you'll pay, and how well you prepare the person for the job." Many of those qualities will apply to other fields as well.

On Australia's Girl.com, an interview with a typical executive personal assistant, a twenty-nine-year-old woman named Fiona Wilson, was posted. "I am the personal assistant to the three directors of a multimedia company. My role can consist of anything from taking minutes to organizing functions or programming a Web site."

"Working as a personal assistant can be a great step to running your own business or working out which field you want to work in without having the qualifications in that field. In my case, my previous PA role was for a small business and I learnt the whole business back to front. Essentially I can apply that to any role I want or establish my own business. In this role now I have learnt how bigger corporations work and the importance of procedures and foundations for setting up a successful company."

"I love the challenge of the day. You never know what might land in my tray. For instance last week I organized a proposal for a Web site, booked training sessions for clients, held two client training sessions, wrote and sent a weekly newsletter to our members, did HTML and Lotus Notes programming to update our Web site, went to a fashion launch for a client, took minutes at four board meetings, organized a breakfast function, organized a promotion for one of our Web sites, finalized printing requirements for a client, prepared staff manuals for the new recruits, sent RSVPs for the directors to attend functions, and so on…"

"The best advice I can give is great communication and time management are the foundations for anywhere you want to go. Understanding how everything works makes you a good boss for the future."

PREPARING FOR YOUR CAREER

A good personal assistant has a take-charge personality, likes to keep things moving, and can usually see what's coming up a day, a week, or a month down the road. They like to be in control. To prepare for a job as a personal assistant, high school students are encouraged to take English, speech, communications, math, sociology, history, typing, bookkeeping, and computer classes. Above all, you need to be organized. Having experience with computers, various types of software (both PC and Macintosh), knowledge of MS Office, and a good handle on time management is essential. You also need basic secretarial skills and a lot of creativity (especially when you are assisting multiple people who all want things done as a priority). Statistics show that time spent successfully managing extracurricular activities such as athletic teams, scouting troops, and community fund-raisers can help young people develop the types of skills they will one day need as personal or executive assistants.

Terrific phone skills are important for an administrative assistant. You field calls for yourself and your employer, often following specific rules.

SALARY EXPECTATIONS AND JOB OUTLOOK

The 2015 median salary for administrative assistants/secretaries in the United States was $36,500. With 3.9 million administrative assistants in 2014, the position is seen as one that will not vanish anytime soon and one that is an excellent place to begin one's career.

Working as a personal assistant is job that has seen much growth over the past decade. And with the growing complexities of everyday life, more and more people with means have come to rely upon organized individuals to help them plan their professional and personal lives.

The book *Beyond the Red Carpet: Keys to Becoming a Successful Personal Assistant* by Dionne M. Muhammad asserts, "These machines of modern business are a hybrid of secretary, project manager and confidante to their employer. Personal assistants are demanding more responsibility, autonomy, and recognition." And in her view, they're getting it.

In a *Los Angeles Times* article, one celebrity assistant's job was assessed as follows: "No longer are personal assistants simply gofers, those harried folks who appear just outside the paparazzo's frame, usually bedraggled and weighed down by luggage. They have begun to organize. They have formed associations in New York and Los Angeles. They have written how-to books and established training programs, even internships."

"In the past, people became personal assistants right out of college, for lack of a better option or because their job in show business eventually led them to one needy celebrity. Today young people are lining up to apply for the jobs that they have seen in action on any number of unscripted TV shows." To be sure, being a personal assistant can be both interesting and rewarding.

FOR MORE INFORMATION

ORGANIZATIONS

American Management Association
1601 Broadway
New York, NY 10019
(877) 566-9441
Website: http://www.amanet.org
This organization provides training and support to
individuals in administrative and management
positions.

The Association of Executive and Administrative
Professionals (AEAP)
900 S. Washington Street, Suite G-13
Falls Church, Virginia 22046
(703) 237-8616
Website: http://www.theaeap.com
This network is by and for administrative professionals,
providing career support and new opportunities.

National Management Association
2210 Arbor Boulevard
Dayton, Ohio 45439
(937) 294-0421

Website: http://www.nma1.org
This professional organization provides support to
potential managers, giving them the tools they need
to increase their potential.

BOOKS

Burge, Joan, Nancy Fraze, and Jasmine Freeman. *Who
Took My Pen...Again? Secrets from Dynamic Executive
Assistants.* Las Vegas, NV: Office Dynamics, 2013.
Stroman, James, Kevin Wilson, and Jennifer Wauson.
Administrative Assistant's and Secretary's Handbook.
New York, NY: AMACOM, 2014.

WEBSITES

Because of the changing nature of internet links, Rosen
Publishing has developed an online list of websites
related to the subject of this book. This site is updated
regularly. Please use this link to access the list:

http://www.rosenlinks.com/CCWC/planning

CHAPTER 4

ORGANIZER

People who live cluttered lives often wish they knew how to get organized and simplify the mess. Others see the problem and immediately know how to best get things under control. It's those people who may find a career as a professional organizer.

Accountemps, a temporary staffing service, conducted a survey and concluded that corporate executives waste five weeks of each year trying to locate missing items. Homeowners probably spend as much, if not more, time doing the same thing.

WHAT THEY DO

Professional organizers are usually hired by home owners or companies to come into a home or business, assess the situation, coordinate the organization effort, and then create a strategy for maintaining order. Sometimes organizational problems can be solved in a single day, but most problems

A cluttered living space can affect everything from day-to-day activities to overall mental well-being. An organizer can help clear the clutter and create a plan for staying organized in the long-term.

that require a professional need several days if not weeks to get things under control.

An organizer will concentrate on controlling clutter, helping to develop filing systems for papers, important documents, photographs, and media. Other personal items such as clothing, cosmetics, linens, and collectibles also need to be made orderly. Personal organizers can examine an existing space and help maximize its potential, creating a personalized storage system that suits his or her client's lifestyle.

Organizedtimes.com's website points out, "Regardless of their background, all successful 'veteran' organizers share certain characteristics—a passion for organizing principles, a strong set of people skills, the ability to teach new ideas to people, sharply honed 'problem-solving' skills, and the ability to organize their own business dealings. But don't worry if you feel lacking in some of these areas—becoming an organizer is a continual process of growing, so you will acquire these skills as you grow and evolve."

PREPARING FOR A CAREER

Some organizations, like the National Association of Professional Organizers, offer certification for professional organizers. Noncertified professional organizers have to work hard to develop a strong reputation in the business, so word of mouth will provide the reputation required to achieve the next assignment.

Many long-established companies offer training services, including the NAPO. These courses can be taught in classrooms, conferences, and even via the Internet. Fees are required and some firms will require first-timers to take their classes before being hired. Some of the topics covered include business basics such as:

- Should I offer a free consultation?
- Should I charge a project fee?
- Should I charge different amounts for consultations and hands-on work?
- Who pays for travel costs?
- When and how should I get paid?
- What do I need to know about preparing proposals for professional work?
- How do I market my services to individuals and corporations?

Additionally, some organizers suggest taking supplemental college or adult-school classes at nearby schools in financial management, writing a business plan, general business, and basic marketing.

Organizations such as the NAPO offer seminars and conferences throughout the year. They also hold a national meeting that rotates locations in different regions throughout the country from year to year.

SALARY EXPECTATIONS

Experienced organizers tend to charge an hourly fee in the $20 to $40 range according to Payscale.com. During the first meeting, the job is assessed and a plan is created. At

Organizers work one-on-one with clients to make a plan. Whether the job is large or small, a good plan is required for success.

that point, an estimate for the number of hours involved is discussed, as well as for materials that are required (storage bins, file folders, whatever may be bought new or acquired from the homeowner to accomplish the goal). Once the client accepts the estimate, some firms ask for a deposit to guarantee a level of commitment from the client. Based on the number of clients taken on, people can earn as little as $500 a month to four times that amount or more.

Ann Gambrell told *Working World* magazine, "Your fee depends on experience. Remember, you are changing someone's life. Some can charge upwards of hundreds of dollars an hour. But most beginners are asking from $25 to $35 an hour. In a few years you can get that to $60, $70, and more, depending on where you live in the country." It's noted by many that fees for work in private homes tend to be less than fees for corporate offices and many organizers maintain separate fee scales for both.

Getting the word out is an important part of the profession. Hollywood-based organizing business the Busy Woman's Daily Planner uses the following advertising methods:

- Emailing two to three times per year
- Direct mailings twice per year
- Phone calls six times per year at minimum
- Contest donations about six times per year
- Coupons in "mom" packs, put in orders or handed out
- Advertisements in trade shows and conventions twice per year
- Offer deals on group discount websites, like Groupon

Jennifer Pacifico, who has run her own organizing business, Wings 4 Organizing, LLC, for seventeen years, offers, "Be consistent. Have great-looking professionally made business cards and avoid a cookie-cutter mentality. Clients are different, and their organizational needs vary a lot from one to the other."

OUTLOOK

The NAPO says that 94 percent of its members are women, mostly working part-time. The field has experienced explosive growth since the mid-1990s. The media has helped promote the field, too, since professional organizers are now being showcased on programs on the Learning Channel and Home & Garden Television. Barry Izsak, president of the NAPO, told Mysanantonio.com, "In all honesty, getting organized isn't rocket science. What we usually see as the reason that people need help is that they feel overwhelmed. A professional organizer helps them step back, look at the situation, analyze it and unlock the mystery, and help them create a process." In many cases, the victims of clutter are people who have unusual attachments to unnecessary items like books, magazines, and newspapers. Other people are just natural collectors who have stepped over the line from manageable to unlivable. Since Americans live in such a consumer-driven culture, the need for personal organizers will likely increase in the next decade. Now is the perfect time to get in on this emerging field.

FOR MORE INFORMATION

ORGANIZATIONS

National Association of Professional Organizers (NAPO)
4700 W. Lake Ave
Glenview, IL 60025
(847) 375-4746
Website: http://napo.net
This is the leading source for organizing and
   productivity professionals, putting them in touch with
   prospective clients.

National Association of Professional Organizers
Los Angeles Chapter
PO Box 50576
Los Angeles, CA 90050
(424) 245-0516
Website: http://www.napola.org
This nonprofit organization is for organizing
   consultants, speakers, trainers, authors, and
   manufacturers of organizing products.

National Association of Professional Organizers,
Washington, DC, Chapter
PO Box 7301

Arlington, VA 22207-0301

(202) 596-2761

Website: http://www.dcorganizers.org

This professional organization for organizing
    professionals, providrd training, seminars, and
    networking opportunities for members.

BOOKS

Hammersley, Toni. *The Complete Book of Home
    Organization.* San Francisco, CA: Weldon Owen, 2016.
Kondo, Marie. *The Life-Changing Magic of Tidying Up:
    The Japanese Art of Decluttering and Organizing.*
    Emeryville, CA: Ten Speed Press, 2014.

WEBSITES

Because of the changing nature of internet links, Rosen
Publishing has developed an online list of websites
related to the subject of this book. This site is updated
regularly. Please use this link to access the list:

http://www.rosenlinks.com/CCWC/planning

CHAPTER 5

PROFESSIONAL FUND-RAISER

People need money in order to survive and to allow commerce to thrive. Some people and organizations need donations from the public and private sectors. This money usually helps finance medical research, sponsors fund-raising activities for special causes, or even helps politicians run for elected office. In just about every case, fund-raisers are needed to champion these needs and causes.

WHAT THEY DO

Professional fund-raisers work for corporations or charities or are members of groups that are hired for special occasions. Fund-raising—an outgrowth of old-fashioned philanthropy—is considered one of the ten largest industries in the United States, according to the *Encyclopedia of Careers and Vocational Guidance*. During 2014, more than $350 billion was raised through charitable giving by public and private donors.

Fund-raising is a cornerstone of American electoral politics. Donors contributed over $240 million to Bernie Sanders's presidential campaign in 2016.

The people who do this work are described by the University of Virginia as "'fund-raising' or 'development,' professionals who research, plan, and carry out strategies to convince individuals, companies, foundations, and governments to donate money to their organizations." Their work varies, depending on the size of the organization. The larger the organization is, the larger its development staff. In cases such as this, each person working on the development staff will have a small function. For instance, an urban hospital usually has a large development staff, while a small nonprofit organization often has a single executive director who oversees the entire fund-raising operation.

Fund-raisers usually focus on one project at a time such as raising money to build a new church or financing the annual running of the Special Olympics. Larger organizations such as the American Heart Association have fund-raising events throughout the year, but the organizers usually run only one campaign at a time. Fund-raising can be done to raise money for education, the environment, health services, the arts, or corporate fund-raising for charities.

A fund-raiser working for a firm will be asked to help with a campaign. The person will meet with the organization to find out the goal of the event, the time-table, and method desired. Research will then be required to examine the reality of the goal, comparing it with the organization's previous efforts, studying the target group of donators, and how the event will be publicized. Then the fund-raiser will study who else will be seeking funds in the same area at the same time. Once compiled, the results become a feasibility study, and from there, a final game plan will be created.

The work itself can vary. Fund-raisers organize a variety of activities that may include raffles, carnivals, phone campaigns, dinners, athletic events, mailings, and even performances. Each of these has to be tailored in some way to the organization and its goal, then planned, advertised, and executed. As a result, the job can be hectic.

Specific tasks include:
- Drawing up budgets, tracking income and expenses, and recording and processing donations
- Writing grant proposals and tracking their progress
- Planning and participating in fund-raising events
- Training and directing volunteers and staff
- Writing publicity materials such as press releases and brochures
- Researching potential donors and developing relation-ships with them
- Attending public events to promote the agency
- Preparing reports and analyses of fund-raising trends and activities

Other times, fund-raisers turn to more sedate approaches to reach the objective. One example of this approach would be setting up a series of talks to focus attention on the problem the money would help address. In some instances, such as in situations that focus on

People walk for a variety of fund-raising events. They walk to help raise money for disease research, including breast cancer, AIDS, and diabetes.

rare diseases or social problems, the public needs to be educated before they are asked for donations.

This is closer to the description of a developer, someone who will develop larger bequests of money, either from philanthropic organizations or wealthy individuals. From there, matching funds from smaller organizations or individuals may be sought.

At Getthatgig.com, a website for young people that lists internship and entry-level job opportunities, they profiled Stephanie Cesna, who was the manager/volunteer coordinator for a recent America's Walk for Diabetes in Chicago. She spent a year planning the event that required her to coordinate all the volunteers and set up registration booths, food tents, sponsor tents, and rest stops during the walk. There were more than one hundred volunteers and more than one thousand participants in the walk. Cesna's goal was to raise $350,000, a number that she met.

"Fund-raising is a very results-driven field," Cesna said. "People who hire fund-raisers want to see that a person is motivated, energetic, and able to prove that they can meet, if not surpass, goals. Often you start at the bottom—possibly as an assistant. This may not sound too exciting, but the learning curve is amazingly fast and the potential to soak up good fund-raising tips is incredible. At my previous job, I was initially just a volunteer coordinator. But I took an interest in the goals of the organization and made an effort to cooperate and assist the director of development. Eventually I was trained and promoted to director of public relations and volunteer development, and invited to participate in fund-raising meetings and task forces. It was a springboard into this job."

PREPARING FOR A CAREER

Money management skills will help you be successful in this field, in addition to accounting skills, public relations savvy, marketing techniques, and the ability to work and communicate with people. To prepare, recommended high school courses include English, creative writing, speech, math, business, history, foreign language, bookkeeping, and computers. Personal skills needed include leadership and enthusiasm, since you're trying to convince people to contribute money to your cause.

You also need to be adaptable since quite often you will be working at the organization's headquarters, which may be cramped or less than ideal. The facilities may be temporary and the hours will certainly be irregular based on the project. A great deal of flexibility will be required for anyone working as a fund-raiser. This is perhaps even more accurate for political fund-raisers than someone working for a community, since candidates cover a district, state, or even the country.

Once you choose to enter this field, it is recommended that you become certified. Certificates are offered by Certified Fund Raising Executive International and need to be renewed every three years.

JOB OUTLOOK AND SALARY

A starting fund-raiser can expect to earn an average of $52,970 a year. An experienced fund-raiser might earn over $100,000. Although professionals generally start

EHow.com, a website of instructional information, offers the following job search tips:

- Search for websites of fund-raising associations and contact the companies for employment information.
- Consult with fund-raisers at large and small fund-raising firms in your area. Ask about the pros and cons of their jobs and for ways to advance in the field.
- Understand that your first few years with a fund-raising organization will be an intensive training period, despite your college degree. You will not be involved in making decisions about any fund-raising drives. Expect your salary to reflect this.
- Receive a professional certification in fund-raising after your have made career advancements. You will raise your status and, possibly, your salary.

out with modest salaries, successful fund-raisers can command significantly higher salaries within just a few years. Even people with only two or three years of experience are likely to earn salaries of $35,000 to $40,000. With five or more years of experience, professionals can earn between $45,000 and $80,000. And senior development executives make salaries of between $75,000 to $140,000.

Job growth surrounding positions in fund-raising is expected to remain robust in the years ahead. Finding the work is not especially difficult. Mark J. Drozdowski writes in the *Chronicle of Higher Education*, "Take time to lurk in development-related chat rooms or bulletin-board sites and you'll find numerous examples of professionals seeking to move from the corporate world to educational fund-raising. Many of them are burned out or dissatisfied with their current lot. Others have lost their jobs or feel unstable in this shaky economy."

While planning a wedding or successful party may be fun and satisfying, many draw a deeper and richer sense of satisfaction knowing their efforts have raised money for noble causes.

FOR MORE INFORMATION

ORGANIZATIONS

Association of Fundraising Professionals
4300 Wilson Boulevardd, Suite 300
Alexandria, VA 22203
(703) 684-0410
Website: http://www.afpnet.org
This organization is dedicated to providing support to
   young fund-raising professionals, ensuring that effective
   and ethical fund-raising is practiced well into the future.

Association of Fundraising Professionals (in Canada)
275 Slater Street, Suite 900
Ottawa, ON K1P 5H9
Canada
(613) 236-0658
Website: http://www.afpnet.org/AFPCanada
This Canada-based organization is for fund-raising
   professionals.

Certified Fund Raising Executive International
225 Reinekers Lane, Suite 625
Alexandria, VA 22314
(703) 820-5555

Website : http://www.cfre.org
This nonprofit organization is dedicated to setting
standards in philanthropy through a valid and reliable
certification process for fund-raising professionals.

BOOKS

Abdalhakim-Douglas, Amal. *Seven Secrets of Successful Fundraising: A Handbook for Both the Professional and New Fundraiser*. Vancouver, BC, Canada: Black Stone Press, 2016.

WEBSITES

Because of the changing nature of internet links, Rosen Publishing has developed an online list of websites related to the subject of this book. This site is updated regularly. Please use this link to access the list:

http://www.rosenlinks.com/CCWC/planning

CHAPTER 6

TRADE SHOW COORDINATOR

Trade show or event coordinators might work for organizations that run trade shows for different corporations, or they work directly for facilities to attract business. There are many different titles that are offshoots of a career in organizing trade shows, such as conference and meeting planner, conference planner, conference services officer, convention coordinator, event planner, festival organizer, meeting planner, special events organizer, or trade-show planner.

WHAT THEY DO

Planners who work for smaller organizations might take full responsibility for an event, while planners on a large staff of a convention bureau might be assigned specific tasks, like budgeting or reservations.

"The massive logistical operation of a large convention, trade show, or expo often starts as many as five years before the event. The first step, booking space in halls and hotels, often must be done years in advance. Then, one or two years before the event, meeting planners begin developing topics, choosing featured speakers, and creating agendas. Much of the work also involves coordinating with other organizations and companies who will present programs and set up booths. Sometimes hundreds of vendors will exhibit their services or products."

Expoweb.com provides a list of responsibilities for trade-show organizers, although not every position requires people to do everything on the list. Conference and event planners perform some or all of the following duties:

- Meet with trade and professional associations and other groups to promote and discuss conference, convention, and trade show services
- Meet with sponsors and organizing committees to plan scope of events, to establish and monitor budgets, and to review administrative procedures and progress
- Coordinate services for events, such as accommodation and transportation for participants, conference and other facilities, catering, signage, displays, translations, special needs requirements, audio-visual equipment, printing, and security

Toy trade show attendees have the chance to see the hottest new toys before they're released and to meet with potential clients.

- Organize registration of participants, prepare programs and promotional materials, and publicize events through local advertisers
- Plan entertainment and social gatherings for participants
- Hire, train, and supervise support staff required for events
- Ensure compliance with required laws
- Negotiate contracts for services, approve suppliers' invoices, maintain financial records, review final billing submitted to clients for events, and prepare reports

Just about every show takes years to plan, whether it's a first-time or a recurring event. The first stop is booking the space. This part can be tricky, especially if the event continues to attract new attendees each year. A space that's too small can kill potential business by overcrowding people and distracting them with too much noise. If a space is too large, the opposite can happen: the vendors and businesses seem paltry and attendance might further decrease. In some cases, the location can expand to accommodate more people, but not every venue has this luxury. Locating a suitable space requires an exact understanding of the client's needs. How much space should be allocated for individual booths? How should booths be spaced apart to accommodate discussions? Will there be an area reserved for food and refreshments? Is there an area needed for registering participants or attendants? Will there be promotional giveaways, a raffle, or other items, such as a guide to the various booths, handed out to attendees? All of these questions and more have to be addressed during the early planning stage.

Once all of these needs are assessed, a suitable space can be reserved. Then a layout of booths is done, and work begins on attracting vendors to display their wares. In many cases, vendors buy booth space at predetermined prices that are based on location. Returning vendors normally get their pick of location and can even receive discounts on the price. Even so, about 40 percent of the vendors miss their critical deadlines, which forces the organizer to keep in touch to make sure everyone is in compliance and steady progress is being made.

The trade-show event staff has to work with the customer to advertise the event within the trade—sometimes both locally and nationally—and then make sure they are equipped to handle first the vendors arriving with their booths and equipment and then the attendees who need to be registered. Planners tend to also be involved in travel arrangements for various participants, so a good familiarity with the internet is a must. Planners must also comply with the Americans with Disabilities Act, since trade shows are required by law to offer access for disabled people. While this may sound simple, a typical booth usually brings its own equipment that needs union crews to assemble, providing it with light, power, phone lines, and Internet connections. Planners must also ensure that each booth meets state fire regulations and that any person, with a disability or not, can enter and exit without trouble. The problems that can come up with the registration process alone are enough to raise the blood pressure of the most sedate trade-show coordinator, so it is a must that he or she be able to keep things running smoothly while under pressure.

During the event itself, which could run from one day to a week, the coordinators attend to last-minute details such

Restaurants and other food vendors meet with suppliers during trade shows in order to help formulate a plan that will increase the cost effectiveness of a business.

as replacing malfunctioning or missing equipment, tracking missing packages, handling complaints from attendees and vendors, and making sure everyone is entertained enough that they will return for the next event.

To perform this job well, people need to have good communications skills, both verbal and written. They also need to think fast on their feet and be ready to handle multiple problems at the same time.

SALARY AND JOB OUTLOOK

According to the Bureau of Labor Statistics, jobs for meeting, convention, and event planners are growing and becoming more available and will continue to do so by about 10 percent until at least 2024. The average salary in 2014 was $46,448.

Thousands of trade and consumer shows take place every year in the United States and Canada. Millions of companies exhibit new products and services at these shows each year. Trade shows and events like them require planning, organization, and publicity.

Careers in trade-show organizing are expected to continue growing in the years ahead. Many municipalities are planning convention or exhibition centers as part of revitalization plans for their communities. On any given day, there are multiple trade shows in major cities around the United States serving professionals from small-business owners to securities workers to restaurant managers.

Sam Bundy, group president for VNU Exposition's ASD/AMD Merchandise Group, sees the trade-show field as a vibrant opportunity for young people. One of the areas he feels is strongly suited for starters is customer service/telemarketing. These are the people who "contact prior attendees of trade shows to facilitate customer needs by providing information and pre-registering them for the next event,"

Bundy says. They also field inbound inquiries for information and/or convention service needs.

For this entry-level position, Bundy stresses that people need good verbal skills, the ability to multitask, a strong work ethic, to enjoy people, and the ability to handle a heavy volume of incoming calls while entering data.

"This starter position is an incubator by providing a platform to learn the business and market," Bundy adds. "Future opportunities are in show operations or sales. I have six employees who started out as customer service representatives who are now in sales or operations. Two of them are senior level managers."

Getting in isn't difficult, and registering with local temporary employment agencies is a good start, Bundy continues. He got into the business through such an agency and at his Las Vegas show, for example, hired fifty temporary staff members. To find a position, Bundy suggests that people contact the human resources departments at trade-show management companies, check out the Internet employment sites for the companies, or join one of the associations for the field. Salaries in this field are competitive.

FOR MORE INFORMATION

ORGANIZATIONS

Convention Industry Council
8201 Greensboro Drive, Suite 300
McLean, VA 22102
(800) 725-8982
Website: http://www.conventionindustry.org
This council supports meeting professionals in order to
ensure a thriving events industry.

Exhibit Designers and Producers Association (EDPA)
19 Compo Road South
Westport, CT 06880
(203) 557-6321
Website: http://www.edpa.com
The EDPA serves thousands of members who work in
the events industry.

Meeting Professionals International (MPI)
International Headquarters
2711 LBJ Freeway, Suite 600
Dallas, TX 75234-7349
(972) 702-3000
Website: http://www.mpiweb.org

This organization fuels the growth and advancement of its members through professional development and career opportunities.

BOOKS

Spark, David. *Three Feet from Seven Figures: One-on-One Engagement Techniques to Qualify More Leads at Trade Shows.* San Francisco, CA: Spark Media Solutions, 2015.

WEBSITES

Because of the changing nature of internet links, Rosen Publishing has developed an online list of websites related to the subject of this book. This site is updated regularly. Please use this link to access the list:

http://www.rosenlinks.com/CCWC/planning

CHAPTER 7

RETAIL MANAGEMENT

What you see when you walk into a store is critical to if and how much money you will spend there. You hope to see that everything is organized and easy to find and that the staff is going to be polite and helpful. Behind a good shopping experience stands a retail manager who brought countless elements together to make the store an inviting place.

The concept of the retail department store began in the latter half of the nineteenth century and it wasn't until the 1930s when chains—which had a single name and uniform look to each store—began growing across the United States.

WHAT THEY DO

Clothing and accessories once dominated retail chains, but in modern times, you can buy almost any type of durable good at a retail chain. As a result, there are several chains in every category adding up to a robust field that is expected, by the US Department of Labor, to continue to grow into the 2020s. One area of growth, electronic commerce via the Internet, is

Retail managers are responsible for handling customer service and employee management. They make schedules, hire new employees, and ensure that every customer has a good experience.

expected to have minimal impact on traditional retail stores while providing a different area of management opportunity.

While cashiers scan merchandise, and sales clerks stock the shelves and greet customers, what exactly what does the manager do? Retail managers hire and train staff, supervise them during operating hours, maintain the physical facilities, manage inventories, monitor expenditures and receipts, and maintain good public relations, not only with every customer but with the neighborhood where the store is located.

A job in retail management comes with high expectations. At job opportunity website Monster.com, Valerie Lipow wrote, "A retail manager's goal is to maximize productivity. This is tough. Store staffs likely include inexperienced, part-time or seasonal employees. Retail hours are long. Sales targets may seem unreachable. Yet, in this setting, good retail managers thrive. They are skilled in four primary areas: managing time, recruiting and supervising staff, building skilled and motivated sales and service teams, and managing change. No manager can be effective in just one of these areas. They are interrelated and interdependent."

With the larger chains, from discount retailers like Wal-Mart to department stores such as Macy's, the corporate leaders dictate how stores are designed, what inventory is to be carried or placed on sale, what promotions will be offered, and even how to decorate for the holidays. Effective managers follow those guidelines to the letter and then add their own touches wherever possible, denoting items that are regional favorites, such as jerseys featuring the name of a local sports team or nearby college. Some chains are stricter than others when it comes to such embellishments, and adhering to those rules will either prolong or curtail a manager's career.

That said, the primary goal of any retail manager is to use all of the above in an effort to maximize overall retail sales. There will be competition to do better than competitive chains or regional stores within the chain.

A constant in the retail business is change. As tastes evolve or new products are introduced, stores need to be adaptable to the whims of the public. As a result, a promotion that worked one holiday may be inappropriate a year later, or a display touting a product may be ignored since people are no longer interested. The retail manager needs to be flexible enough to follow the lead of the customer. If dissatisfied, the customer will shop somewhere else and the manager will face declining sales and unhappy upper management.

For people running their own retail businesses, they can test the pulse of the public and react more quickly, tailoring displays and new product arrivals to the demands of the local population. Here, the retail manager, with a smaller staff and fewer national resources, can compete with the bigger chains by adapting more rapidly to fickle customers.

PREPARING FOR YOUR CAREER

Retail managers must work long hours, show that they are responsible, set a good example to other employees, and practice diplomacy. There are no courses in this field, but English, math, marketing, and economics classes will prove useful to high school students who wish to become retail managers.

A good manager can work his or her way up in a company by showing responsibility and going above and beyond to help fellow employees.

According to the Department of Labor's *Occupational Outlook Handbook*, retail managers are provided training by most of the major chain operations. Practical experience is gained through lower level jobs, but once someone is tapped to become a manager, there is a broader array of subjects that need to be covered. The handbook says, "Classroom training may include such topics as interviewing and customer service skills, employee and inventory management, and scheduling. Management trainees may be placed in one specific department for training on the job, or they may be rotated among several

WORKING YOUR WAY UP

Retail manager Allyn Gibson works for the EB Games chain at a location in Pennsylvania. With five years managerial experience, he began his job as a sales clerk during the summer of 1999 and never left. He notes, "Looking back I made the right choice—I could have spent $26,000 a year attending college or earn $26,000 working in retail. I began as a part-time sales associate, moved into an assistant manager position within three months, and was promoted to store manager a few months later."

Gibson enjoys his job and stresses that experience is the key to becoming a manager. "Responsibilities vary from day to day," Gibson says. "The main duty of an EB employee is to work with customers in determining their needs and selling product[s] to them, but there are store maintenance tasks, such as taking out the garbage, stocking shelves, and cleaning windows and fixtures, that must be done every day. An employee who has demonstrated selling skills, who has shown leadership, and who has proven his or her drive to succeed stands a good chance of being promoted. Retail experience counts, as does sales performance. To be considered for a management position a person needs to demonstrate the ability to drive sales and put money in the cash drawer."

"Retail is very much a 'learn on the job' career—you learn the job by doing the job," Gibson continues. "As a manager I have to examine how well my staff is selling, give them guidance to improve their selling through training and role-playing, and direct them toward completing store operational tasks—like stocking the shelves, processing shipment, and cleaning the store—in a way that balances that against the need to satisfy the customer.

(continued on the next page)

(continued from the previous page)

A manager has to make the store schedule, take care of customer issues, or ship products to other stores or back to the warehouse. Management has a rhythm to it, and that is both an advantage and a disadvantage. Each day is largely like the last. Travel is rare, and you normally spend between forty to fifty hours a week inside the store. "If you work in retail you *will* work weekends, typically every Saturday and one or two Sundays a month. The upshot to working weekends is that days off from work fall in the middle of the week, when banking is done, when the post office is open, when doctors' offices are open, which means that you do not need to take time off from work to do the mundane things in life that need doing."

departments to gather a well-rounded knowledge of the store's operation. Training programs in franchises generally are extensive, covering all functions of the operation, including promotion, marketing, management, finance, purchasing, product preparation, human resource management, and compensation."

JOB OUTLOOK AND SALARY

The national average salary for retail managers is between $43,000-$44,525, according to Glassdoor.com. A district manager can make an average of $72,402 per year, according to Monster.com. Sales managers who work outside of retail can make an average of $113,860, according to the Bureau of Labor Statisics' 2015 findings.

The vast majority of retail store managers achieve their positions after years of work in the retail business, starting as stock clerks or cashiers and rising through the ranks. The average retail worker makes around $22,040 each year, or an average of $10.60 per hour. There are almost five million retail jobs available in the United States, according to the Bureau of Labor Statistics, and because of high turnover in positions like these, companies are usually hiring.

The entire nonretail area of sales management is large and encompasses much not visible to the consumer. A manager in this realm, according to the Department of Labor, is responsible for supervising and coordinating "the activities of sales workers who sell industrial products, automobiles, or services such as advertising or Internet services. They may prepare budgets, make personnel decisions, devise sales-incentive programs, assign sales territories, or approve sales contracts." Like most jobs in the retail sector, jobs in retail management are expected to grow nationally over the next decade, especially in more populated areas.

FOR MORE INFORMATION

ORGANIZATIONS

International Food Service Distributors Association
1410 Spring Hill Road, Suite 210
McLean, VA 22102
(703) 532-9400
Website: http://www.ifdaonline.org
This organization of food service members provides
    support, training, and networking opportunities.

National Automobile Dealers Association
8400 Westpark Drive
Tysons, VA 22102
(800) 821-7000
Website : http://www.nada.org
This network of car dealerships provides support,
    research, guidance, and education to those working
    in the industry.

National Retail Federation (NRF)
325 7th Street NW
Suite 1100
Washington, DC 20004
(800) 673-4692
Website: http://www.nrf.com

NRF is the world's largest retail trade association, representing retailers from the United States and more than forty-five countries.

BOOKS

Berman, Barry, and Joel R. Evans. *Retail Management: A Strategic Approach*, 12th ed. New York, NY: Pearson, 2012.

Levy, Michael, and Barton A. *Weitz. Retailing Management*, 9th ed. New York, NY: McGraw-Hill, 2013.

Reyhle, Nicole, and Jason Prescott. *Retail 101: The Guide to Managing and Marketing Your Retail Business.* New York, NY: McGraw-Hill, 2014.

WEBSITES

Because of the changing nature of internet links, Rosen Publishing has developed an online list of websites related to the subject of this book. This site is updated regularly. Please use this link to access the list:

http://www.rosenlinks.com/CCWC/planning

CHAPTER 8

EVENT COORDINATOR/ EVENT PLANNING

While event coordinator and party planner are different jobs, they encompass many of the same tasks. Event coordinators, however, tend to work on a larger scale and almost exclusively do work for corporations. For example, there is approximately $80 billion a year spent on these events according to the Professional Conference Management Association.

WHAT THEY DO

There are currently around 100,000 event planner-related jobs in the United States, according to the Department of Labor Statistics. It breaks the field into three sections: "In workplaces with several meeting planners, three levels of professionalism exist: the facilitator, the technician, and the professional. The facilitator may be assigned basic tasks such as choosing menus and working with the hotel on a variety of details. A person holding this position is concerned with the physical needs of the attendees. The technician is often responsible for running registration and reservations,

Event planners meet with clients to determine their needs. Every event needs a plan that is executed well.

selecting and setting up the site, and operating the budget. The professional designs and sells the event, creates the budget, and oversees all operations. It is this top-level manager who is responsible for achieving the meeting's overall objective: the communication goal of the client."

What is an event? It could be the halftime show at the Super Bowl or it could be an off-site training session for corporate managers. It usually involves a special occasion, away from the office, and quite often involves the general public.

Planning and budgeting for these events usually takes weeks, if not months, involving invitations, advertising, visiting various sites, arranging for meals or staffing, and figuring out the entertainment and other creative ways to effectively communicate the client's message. Many of these events mean interfacing with counterparts at the site, or with people in related fields such as catering, florists, media communications, and corporate officials.

When an event is needed, perhaps the company picnic or the introduction of a new product, the in-house planners are consulted. For many companies, they turn to independent planning companies to handle the arrangements. At the first meeting, the parameters of the event are outlined, including such details as the timing and location.

The first thing the event coordinator is likely to do is check the calendars of the major corporate officers to make sure they are free and clear to attend. If the event is a product launch, the event coordinator needs to ensure that that product is on schedule. If a space is needed, one is located and reserved. Once the space is chosen, the rest of the arrangements can follow. The coordinator may be required to establish a guest list, determine if registration is required, and if so, how to process that information (by phone, mail, fax, or internet).

To handle all of the details, the coordinator must be good at record keeping, financial negotiating, and have excellent communication skills. Because he or she is the intermediary between the company and all of the vendors providing the

MICHAEL T. FIUR PRODUCTIONS

When Michael T. Fiur's career took off, he had no idea it would lead him to working as a producer. After graduating from college, he stayed in Binghamton, New York, to organize a mayoral race, which he helped win, and then served on the mayor's staff. The hurly-burly lifestyle and constant planning of events over six years inspired him to become a large-scale event coordinator/producer.

President of Michael T. Fiur Productions, Fiur is a leading producer of events in the United States. After leaving politics, he moved home to New York City and began working with Madison Square Garden's entertainment division before a ten-year stint at Radio City Music Hall. While there, he worked on five Super Bowl halftime shows, six productions of the Radio City Christmas Spectacular, and numerous corporate and civic events. All that experience inspired him to form his own company. His experience also landed the contracts to produce Arthur Ashe Kids' Day each year and all the entertainment for the US Open. Fiur is currently developing an off-Broadway musical called *Superstar*.

"As a live event/television and theatrical producer, I view my role as the 'glue' that holds it all together," he explains. "I am responsible for managing the budget, hiring the creative team, overseeing the creative process, holding the client's hand, and seeing the show through to successful completion. My two rules of producing are to create a truly memorable experience for the audience, and stay on budget."

various services that will support the event, courteous and responsive communication is extremely important. Creative thinking will be required in making an initial presentation to a client. Creativity also comes into play when making the event come to life and when inevitable problems occur. The coordinator's job can be hectic and noisy and filled with long days, especially as the event date looms, many of which will be spent with a cell phone in hand at all times.

PREPARING FOR YOUR CAREER

To prepare for a career as an event coordinator, your high school courses should include English, business, speech, and

The hospitality industry is one that can provide a great start for a lot of different careers. You deal with all types of customer service needs.

a foreign language. Summer jobs working in the hospitality industry—at hotels, restaurants, and resorts—will also help.

Other possibilities to gain related experience might be found by volunteering at your local office of tourism. Once in the field, you should get certified through the organization Meeting Professionals International, which is listed in the directory at the end of this chapter.

Corporations, hotels, and convention centers often have their own planning staff as well as employees from private companies that provide similar services. As a result, once you enter the event-planning field, there are many opportunities to learn, and possibly some to advance your career. Employees can advance to positions in management, quite often promoted from within, or drafted from one company to another. Recruiting is a standard practice in event-planning fields. Cross recruiting may also bring people to travel companies and museums.

To start in the field, an internship at places such as convention bureaus and exhibition centers is a great opportunity to gain experience. The Department of Labor, notes, however, that "although experience can be gained by arranging weddings and catering parties for acquaintances or family members, this type of experience alone is rarely sufficient to be hired as a corporate meeting planner without having a broader work history in event planning and obtaining certification." There is also a growing field of course work at colleges under their hotel management programs for people who want to learn more about the business. Once you are in the field, successful planners attend annual seminars, workshops, conventions, and trade meetings while also reading trade journals and browsing websites to stay ahead of trends.

JOB OUTLOOK AND SALARY

Salaries for event coordinators are usually between $23,000 and $42,000, with a national average salary of $35,000, according to Glassdoor.com. Salaries for event planners range from between $26,000 and $80,000, according to the Department of Labor, with the higher end being represented by corporate event planning.

Event coordinators and planners may work in both the public and private sectors. In the long term, opportunities in the event-planning fields are available and growing. In the past decade, more and more corporations are outsourcing their event-planning and promotional needs to independent contractors. Event coordinators might be hired by a variety of firms including hotel chains, educational institutions, corporations, convention centers, municipal parks, and tourism associations. In addition, many event coordinators with experience can cross over into a host of related careers such as those in public relations, hospitality management, or even organizing the catering and social functions of film and television production companies.

FOR MORE INFORMATION

ORGANIZATIONS

Convention Industry Council
8201 Greensboro Drive, Suite 300
McLean, VA 22102
(800) 725-8982
Website: http://www.conventionindustry.org
The CIC's thirty-three member organizations represent over 103,500 individuals and 19,500 firms and properties involved in the meetings, conventions, and exhibitions industry.

Meeting Professionals International (MPI)
2711 LBJ Freeway, Suite 600
Dallas, TX 75234-7349
(972) 702-3000
Website: http://www.mpiweb.org
The MPI fuels the growth and advancement of MPI members by providing them professional development and career opportunities through grants and scholarships.

BOOKS

Capell, Laura. *Event Management for Dummies.* Hoboken, NJ: For Dummies, 2013.

Kilkenny, Shannon. *The Complete Guide to Successful Event Planning*, 2nd ed. Ocala, FL: Atlantic Publishing, 2011.

Kimball, Cheryl. *Start Your Own Event Planning Business: Your Step-By-Step Guide to Success.* Irvine, CA: Entrepreneur Press, 2015.

Malouf, Lena. *Events Exposed: Managing and Designing Special Events.* Hoboken, NJ: Wiley, 2012.

Roney, Carley. *The Knot Ultimate Wedding Planner & Organizer: Worksheets, Checklists, Etiquette, Calendars, and Answers to Frequently Asked Questions.* New York, NY: Potter Craft, 2013.

MAGAZINES

Meeting Professional
3030 LBJ Freeway, Suite 1700
Dallas, TX 75234-2759
(972) 702 3000
Website: http://www.mpiweb.org

Meeting Professional magazine is a publication of
Meeting Professionals International, the largest
meeting and event industry association worldwide.

WEBSITES

Because of the changing nature of internet links, Rosen
Publishing has developed an online list of websites
related to the subject of this book. This site is updated
regularly. Please use this link to access the list:

http://www.rosenlinks.com/CCWC/planning

CHAPTER 9

MERCHANDISE PLANNER/ ASSISTANT PLANNER

Most retail sales operations have employees called merchandise planners who determine the perfect product mix to place in each store, help figure out which vendors to buy goods from, and how to maximize regional differences for optimum sales. It's the ultimate organizing opportunity within a retail environment!

WHAT THEY DO

Merchandise planners are responsible for developing an initial financial strategy for sales, markdowns, and profit. They have to project into the future and make an educated guess about what people will want to buy in specific product categories from bath towels to TVs. Within each product category there may be subset categories that also need analysis. These strategies must be considered for all retail stores, taking geographic differences into account as well as determining the content for a retail business's print catalogue and/or virtual internet business.

Throughout the year, the planner will study the marketplace and the competition to make course corrections for the existing selling year and then modify those projections for the next sales cycle (some sales cycles change seasonally, not annually, such as clothing).

Once the plan is made, it then needs to be implemented in retail outlets around the state, nation, or world. Planners work with an array of computerized tools to help determine sales trends as well as how long it takes manufacturers to assemble required items so there's never a shortage. Sometimes there are delays, known as back orders, and they need to be addressed quickly, otherwise customers will leave the store in frustration and possibly never return.

Planners do not work in a vacuum since they often do the actual buying and are in touch with managers who oversee stock replenishment. Still, the planner makes a point of maximizing every square inch of a store in order to excite customers and increase sales.

Quite often, planners from large retail stores such as Wal-Mart or Sears rely on a tool known as a planogram, which is a schematic drawing of the store.

Merchandise planning for large stores, like Sears, is more involved and complicated than that done at smaller stores and boutiques.

From there, the planner will allocate a large amount of shelf space for one item and possibly less for another. These act as the blueprints for the store managers to follow when instructing employees how to stock the shelves. The planner determines the most logical approach for placing related items together. Socks are placed near undergarments, for example. The planner also needs to consider who the suppliers are and with whom the company has exclusive or specific deals since some manufacturers receive preferential treatment over a competitor, which often means they receive more shelf space. It's all a giant puzzle for the planner and one that needs to be rebuilt throughout the year or, in the case of supermarkets, almost weekly. Some planners will allow for regional differences, too, allowing store managers to make some product placement choices on their own since they know the local shoppers best.

"The planograms—or modulars—make sense insofar as everything fits in the space allotted. Each set is actually constructed at the home office before it reaches the stores. And the layout pages have always explicitly stated that they are 'only a guide' and can be adjusted according to a given store's clientele and needs," notes John Wells, a manager in one of Wal-Mart's Iowa locations.

"The store planners do tour a certain amount of stores in a given year, but the sheer number of Wal-Marts means they'll only visit a fraction of them. The buyers are available by phone and e-mail."

The planner usually works as part of a team with assistants who may be responsible for individual product categories such as notions in a crafts store or socks in a clothing store. The Dollar General chain, for example, has a team of five planners for its nearly seven thousand stores in the United States.

Bed Bath & Beyond requires planners to possess "business knowledge of retail and merchandising concepts and strong problem-solving and analytical skills. Knowledge of planning and allocation systems [is also encouraged]." A London retail firm described its planning position as one that would allow applicants to "develop planning and forecasting skills…[and] be heavily involved in long-range planning and customer insight."

PREPARING FOR YOUR CAREER

Prior retail experience is really helpful to have in order to perform this job well, especially in store planning, inventory management, financial planning, or financial analysis. Retail management or sales skills do not seamlessly allow for people to enter this field. Many of the larger chains, such as Federated, offer employees training programs, helping them develop the analytic skills to enhance their skills.

JOB OUTLOOK AND SALARY

Merchandise planners are usually hired as hourly employees and are then eventually promoted to fill the merchandise-planning role as they advance. Geographic variance makes it difficult to determine average salaries, however. Upscale retail chains will pay between $63,000 and $85,000 for experienced planners.

Home decor and improvement, as at Bed Bath & Beyond, are both retail sectors that continue to grow and make money over time. A good merchandise planner knows how to keep that momentum going.

Jobs in merchandise planning have a strong future over the next decade. A wise choice for most people looking to get a job with a solid company is to examine its progress over a given period. Obviously it's more desirable to work as a planner for a store that has a strong future. Do your research. Is it a *Fortune* 500 company? Does it have a strong market share and a positive image? Bed Bath & Beyond is just one example of a company that expects a good deal of growth over the next few years.

FOR MORE INFORMATION

ORGANIZATIONS

Center for Retailing Studies
Texas A&M University
Department of Marketing
201 Wehner Building
4112 TAMU
College Station, TX 77843-4112
(979) 845-0325
Website: http://mays.tamu.edu/center-for-retailing-studies
This Texas A&M study program is dedicated to retail
    education and business.

National Retail Federation (NRF)
Liberty Place
325 7th Street NW, Suite 1100
Washington, DC 20004
(202) 783-0370
Website: http://www.nrf.com
NRF is the world's largest retail trade association,
    representing retailers from the United States and
    more than forty-five countries.

Retail Design Institute
126A West 14th Street

2nd floor
Cincinnati, OH 45202
(513) 751-5815
Website: https://www.retaildesigninstitute.org
This institute promotes the advancement
    and collaborative practice of creating
    selling environments.

BOOKS

Fisher, Marshall, and Ananth Raman. *The New Science of Retailing: How Analytics Are Transforming the Supply Chain and Improving Performance*. Watertown, MA: Harvard Business Publishing, 2010.

WEBSITES

Because of the changing nature of internet links, Rosen Publishing has developed an online list of websites related to the subject of this book. This site is updated regularly. Please use this link to access the list:

http://www.rosenlinks.com/CCWC/planning

CHAPTER 10

AUCTIONEER

Before online auctions existed on the internet, through sites like Ebay, interested buyers met in person to put bids on a variety of items. People have been auctioning goods for centuries and the job of auctioneer remains a thriving career opportunity, even today.

WHAT THEY DO

Auctioneers must be well informed about an item and the history of its market value before the responsibilities of speaking very fast and forcing the price of an item higher. Some auctioneers sell antiques, others sell art, and still others sell agricultural equipment or used cars.

The auctioneer prepares for many hours before the day of the event. He or she is responsible for the appraisal of goods, assembling them, and then advertising the auction. In many cases, such as when entire estates are sold at auction, the auctioneer works closely with the family, company, or agency to maximize the value of the estate's contents.

The National Auctioneers Association states, "The single most important role an auctioneer takes on is that of marketing expert. Auctioneers are adept at marketing a client's property through the appropriate media and reaching a specific audience. In large part, their livelihood depends upon being able to attract those individuals most interested, and therefore, most willing to buy a particular item. The ability to market auctions and merchandise effectively comes from an intimate knowledge of the specific types of merchandise, its value, the demand for such merchandise, and the targeted market."

"Beyond being able to juggle a number of duties, the prospective auctioneer needs to be personable and work well with a variety of people. During the course of organizing a sale, the auctioneer consults with the seller, fields questions from potential buyers and, on occasion, mediates disputes."

When an auctioneer is hired to handle a sale, his or her first task is to review the items and prepare an evaluation for the seller. The items for sale begin with a "reserved" price, meaning the minimum price for bidding to start. In some cases, it is decided there should no minimum and then bidding begins with an "absolute" price. This step is the most time consuming and requires a level of expertise in a number of areas. Some auctioneers specialize in livestock, wine, or fine art, for example. Some auction houses

Christie's is one of the best-known auction houses in the world. It specializes in antiques and priceless art.

are famous, too, such as Christie's and Sotheby's, which have become noteworthy for their high-end art, collectibles, and precious gems.

While reviewing the items, the auctioneer notes the history, background, and condition of the item, information to not only determine the reserved price, but which will also be used during the auction itself.

Once the evaluation is done, the timing and venue for the event must be determined. Not every auction is done at an auction house. Some are done on farm sites, at rodeos, in concert or sports stadiums, or anywhere a large crowd can gather comfortably. Some states even auction off stolen vehicles, which require a huge amount of space for display and handling.

After the venue is selected, an auction can be advertised. This can start with ads in newspapers or flyers, or it can go all the way up to pricey catalogues. Here, the order of items is determined and the auctioneer carefully sets the pacing of the auction so the most valuable or most unique items go on the block later, keeping people on hand to view the entire auction. It is also important for the auctioneer to maintain control over the auction's tempo and organization in order to maximize sales.

On the day of the auction, the auctioneer welcomes people to the event, allows potential buyers to take a closer look at the items for sale, and surveys the attitude of the crowd. He or she must be careful to control the flow of the event, adjusting the speed as required. As a result, one of the best qualities an auctioneer can have is a quick-thinking mind to anticipate what changes are necessary before they are needed. The audience must be kept interested and entertained by the patter of information at all times.

Other skills recommended for would-be auctioneers include having a strong, clear voice, and a friendly, confident manner. Auctioneers must be able to work with customers and tactfully advise them on an item's value. He or she must have a wide knowledge of the types of goods that are being auctioned,

FREQUENTLY HEARD TERMS AT AUCTIONS

ABSENTEE BID A procedure that allows a person called an absentee bidder to participate in the bidding process without being physically present.

AGENT A person who acts for or in the place of another individual or entity by authority from the individual or entity.

APPRAISAL The act or process of estimating value.

AUCTION BLOCK The podium or platform where the auctioneer stands while conducting the auction.

BID A prospective buyer's offer of a price he or she will pay to purchase property at auction. Bids are usually in standardized increments established by the auctioneer.

CAVEAT EMPTOR A Latin phrase meaning "let the buyer beware." A legal maxim stating that the buyer takes the risk regarding quality or condition of the property purchased.

DUE DILIGENCE The process of gathering information about the condition and legal status of assets to be sold.

HAMMER PRICE The price established by the last bidder and acknowledged by the auctioneer before dropping the hammer.

OPENING BID The first bid offered by a bidder at an auction.

SEALED BID A method of sale utilized where confidential bids are submitted and later opened at a predetermined place and time.

as well as a good visual memory, and a strong business sense in order to understand the legal aspects of the work in detail.

PREPARING FOR YOUR CAREER

If you're interested in gaining experience as an auctioneer, you might want to gain experience on a volunteer basis at your high school or church. There are many family-run auction businesses and they usually accept entry-level people, starting them in the office and having them learn by assisting current auctioneers. Most auctioneers start out as part-timers, learning their craft and their specialties.

There are also numerous schools that issue certificates through the National Auctioneers Association. Different states have different licensing requirements, which should be checked when seeking employment. At least twenty-seven states require certification, while at least fifty require real estate auctioneers to be licensed. Also, most auctioneers follow the National Auctioneers Association's rules of conduct that enable an auctioneer to earn the trust of a seller. The NAA's website adds, "Often licensing boards will waive the educational credits if an applicant served as an apprenticeship under a licensed auctioneer. Required apprenticeships can range in length from conducting a few auctions under an auctioneer's guidance to one or more years."

The Florida Auctioneer Academy's website notes, "Public speaking, leadership background and marketing experience are useful in developing presentation skills.

Technology is rapidly moving into the industry, with computerized clerking and fax marketing, as well as online marketing."

JOB OUTLOOK AND SALARY

While most auctioneers work on their own, larger auctions will use assistants called ringmen, either to display items to an audience or to take down bids from the crowd and bring them to the auctioneer. Salaries can vary, but most auctioneers make their money through commissions.

As the sale ends, the auctioneer sees to it that the items are delivered to the proper buyer and that the agreed-upon price has been paid. In some cases this may mean arranging shipping, transport, or careful wrapping for items that were auctioned that day.

For these services, most auctioneers receive an increase in commission, usually a percentage of the total sale that was previously agreed upon. According to Schmoop.com, the average salary for an auctioneer is around $46,000. Real estate or art auctioneers might be paid up to $250,000 for certain companies.

More than two dozen schools teach the skills required for a career in auctioneering. Most every state has a

Antiques auctioneers must stay informed about what items are worth so they can fetch the best price for a seller. A scratch or other flaw on the item will bring down the value.

professional organization to oversee auctioneers in their area. While no statistics on career growth are available, given America's current interest in auctions fueled by the success of eBay, this is likely to be a robust career option in the years ahead.

FOR MORE INFORMATION

ORGANIZATIONS

Auctioneers Association of Ontario
30959 Wyatt Road RR #6
Strathroy, ON N7G 3H7
Canada
(519) 232-4138
Website: http://auctioneersassociation.com
The Auctioneers Association of Ontario is a volunteer
   group of professionals who strive to bring consistency
   and sound business practices to the auction industry.

National Auctioneers Association (NAA)
8880 Ballentine
Overland Park, KS 66214
(913) 541-8084
Website: http://www.auctioneers.org
NAA is the world's largest professional association
   dedicated to auction professionals.

Sotheby's Auction House
1334 York Avenue
New York, NY 10021
(212) 606-7000
Website: http://www.sothebys.com

This global auction company sells items for businesses and private clients.

BOOKS

Bradley, Sandy. *Benefit Auctions: A Fresh Formula for Grassroots Fundraising*. Sarasota, FL: Pineapple Press, 2015.

WEBSITES

Because of the changing nature of internet links, Rosen Publishing has developed an online list of websites related to the subject of this book. This site is updated regularly. Please use this link to access the list:

http://www.rosenlinks.com/CCWC/planning

CHAPTER 11

OPERATIONS MANAGER/ TRAFFICKER

Almost everything that is manufactured and sold is made up of many parts, and the coordination of these parts—acquiring them, assembling them, and making them available for sale—requires a high degree of coordination. In different fields, this job title is known as either trafficker, or more commonly, operations manager.

WHAT THEY DO

A good operations manager is the secret to success for almost every busy company. They ensure that businesses run smoothly. They establish schedules, projecting when fresh materials will be required. They also coordinate the shipping of materials, and can handle production schedules, manpower schedules, and many other functions that keep companies on track. Some of the positions that fall under the field of operations management include assembly-line workers, mail-room operations, supply-chain managers, and much more. Operations professionals understand how each department is just one cog in the wheel of a larger corporation. They are people who work behind the scenes making sure that each area of a corporation functions as well as it could.

When looking at companies for work, study how they're organized. You'll find that each one has one or more departments dedicated to communicating between departments, shipping and receiving goods, and making things run as smoothly as possible. The entry-level positions are usually clerical or assistant managers, responsible for a small piece of the puzzle. As people gain experience, they gain greater responsibility for the overall operation of the company. Senior operations people tend to be part of senior management. They are normally involved in decisions, such as where the company is based, how facilities

Operations managers interact between departments in order to keep a company running smoothly.

should be constructed or modified, and how new technologies can be integrated to improve workflow and production.

The operations department is vital to any company. Operations managers usually bear the brunt of some tedious work, with long hours and many problems that need immediate solving. "Operations" is an all-encompassing term, which, depending upon the size and scope of the company, may include positions in customer service, sales, accounting, logistics, production, and maintenance. Operations managers exist to support the company and its goals to produce the best possible goods in the shortest possible time. This can mean adjusting work schedules or finding better vendors for supplies.

PREPARING FOR YOUR CAREER

Many companies do require an employee to have a business degree or MBA, but some will hire people in the lower ranks if they can prove they have the problem-solving skills and personality to handle challenges. Once hired an employee will develop skills and experience that are usually taught in classes. The skills usually sought for this position include not only an understanding of processes, but of people. Operations managers need to demonstrate strong leadership, sharp analytical skills, and excellent communication skills, both written and verbal. Another key element is building a team that can follow directions and work toward a common goal. Operations managers always work with a team, so good interpersonal skills are vital. High school students should take courses in English, math, computers, and even public speaking.

JOB OUTLOOK AND SALARY

Salaries vary by region, profession, and official job title, so averages can fall anywhere between $40,000 and $110,000. Most operations managers start as hourly employees and move into salaried positions through promotion. Also, since most operations people are promoted from within the company, it's a career that promises greater advancement than other jobs surveyed in this book. The Virginia Labor

Excellent communication skills can take you a long way in a career as an operations manager.

Department says, "Career success is both about what you do (applying your technical knowledge, skills, and ability) and how you do it (the consistent behaviors you demonstrate and choose to use) while interacting and communicating with others."

The field of operations management is seen as a growing one given the challenges companies face through increased international competition. With changing technology as well as the evolving marketplace, operations managers will succeed by staying on top of these changes as they pertain to their chosen profession. According to the US Bureau of Labor Statistics, projected employment growth for top-level operations managers varies by industry; however, keen competition is expected for these positions because the prestige and high pay attract a large number of qualified applicants.

FOR MORE INFORMATION

ORGANIZATIONS

Institute of Certified Professional Managers (ICPM)
James Madison University
MSC 5504
Harrisonburg, VA 22807
(800) 586-4120
Website: http://cob.jmu.edu/icpm
With over 12,000 managers and leaders certified
worldwide, the Institute of Certified Professional
Managers is the largest management certifying body
in the United States, doing business globally.

National Management Association
2210 Arbor Boulevard
Dayton, Ohio 45439
(937) 294-0421
Website: http://www.nma1.org/
Headquartered in Dayton, Ohio, NMA is a
national, not-for-profit organization serving
thousands of customers in leadership positions
worldwide, providing support to people in
management positions.

BOOKS

Belker, Loren B., Jim McCormick, and Gary S. Topchik. *The First-Time Manager*. New York, NY: AMACOM, 2013.
Buckingham, Marcus, and Curt Coffman. *First, Break All the Rules: What the World's Greatest Managers Do Differently*. Washington, DC: Gallup Press, 2016.

WEBSITES

Because of the changing nature of internet links, Rosen Publishing has developed an online list of websites related to the subject of this book. This site is updated regularly. Please use this link to access the list:

http://www.rosenlinks.com/CCWC/planning

CHAPTER 12

CORPORATE TRAVEL COORDINATOR

Travel coordinators make a plan to get a person, family or group from one place to another safely and with minimal fuss. They also work hard to make the trip an enjoyable experience. The travel coordinator or travel agent is the person people turn to for their travel needs. Travel coordinators and agents either work from home, for an agency, or for a major firm.

More and more, companies that use travel as part of their daily operation hire an in-house staff to effectively control pricing and services. As a result, the corporate travel coordinator is a small but growing field. Traditional travel agents have struggled over the past few years given the rise of internet travel sites and the rise of competitive pricing services such as Expedia.com, Priceline.com, and Travelocity.com. Filling the gaps is the independent travel coordinator, someone working independently either in a small office or out of his or her home.

The Minnesota Department of Labor notes, "Airlines no longer pay commissions to travel agencies, which has reduced revenues and caused some agencies to go out of business. However, many consumers still prefer to use a

Companies that require a lot of travel from their employees often hire a travel coordinator to handle the details.

professional travel agent to ensure reliability, to save time, and, in some cases, to save money."

PREPARING FOR YOUR CAREER

There are a variety of skills required for a travel coordinator to be successful. Since all travel arrangements are now made electronically, good computer skills top the list of qualifications. Those who wish to enter this field should also be excellent communicators since you will be writing or speaking with customers each day. If you run your own service, good math and business skills are also necessary. If you already take classes in a foreign language, you'll be even more qualified when the time comes. Obviously, you also need to have a good handle on world geography as well.

There are two primary computer software programs used by agents to make hotel, plane, and other travel arrangements. These computer skills are usually taught at training programs that you may be required to take before beginning work in this field. Vocational schools and private firms also offer these courses.

Once at work, agents and coordinators tend to sit at desks or behind counters and field telephone calls or walk-in customers looking to travel. Quite often the customer has only a vague idea of when and where they want to go and the amount of money they can spend to accomplish the trip. The agent will then explore the options and help shape the customer's goals. There are others, however, especially business travelers, who might have exact specifications such as where they need to be and when. In this case, the agent has to match those specifications with the best possible deal. With competing airlines, hotels, package tours, and more, the agent needs to help the customer sift through his or her options. Agents will also be called upon to help travelers solve problems once the trip has begun, which may include a plane breaking down and stranding the customer in the wrong city. As a result, patience is one of the most important job skills a travel agent needs.

Professional travel coordinators can often handle their duties from home, over the phone, through email, or by text.

For those who prefer to work independently, the personal touch will bring in new business and return customers. For example, an agent sometimes works from his or her home and drums up business by coming up with incentive trips companies can offer employees as rewards or bonuses.

JOB OUTLOOK AND SALARY

The Department of Labor reports that nationally, the average salary for travel agents is $35,660 per year ($17.15 per hour).

TRAVELS IN PHARMACEUTICALS

At Pfizer, one of America's leading pharmaceutical firms, Philip Dunphy is a director of global travel services, seeing that the company gets its people to and from locations around the world safely and economically. With his staff, Dunphy is on the phone constantly looking for the best deals and arrangements for a chemist going to a new lab in a foreign city or a research analyst who is bringing a hundred corporate executives from all points of the globe to a single place for a meeting.

Dunphy notes that people can get into this field without a college degree, usually training under someone who is an experienced and certified agent. They need to know computer reservation systems, either the Apollo or Sabre programs, and be very comfortable with computers and the Internet. "Excellent verbal communication skills to effectively handle phone requests" are a must, Dunphy insists. Customer service and knowledge of geography are always seen as pluses on job applications.

"The ability to work in a fast-paced environment and handle multiple requests simultaneously is essential," Dunphy explains. "If you have the ability to defuse upset travelers and resolve problems expeditiously, you're on your way."

Certainly these figures could increase if an agent or coordinator works independently from an agency.

According to the Minnesota Department of Labor, "The travel industry is sensitive to economic downturns because fewer people go on vacation during these periods. Therefore, the number of job opportunities for travel agents varies with the state of the economy." And the United States Department of Labor sees a 12 percent reduction in traditional travel agents through 2024. The combined number of travel agents who work for an agency and those who work from home is around one hundred thousand, per an article on Travelweekly.com from 2013.

FOR MORE INFORMATION

ORGANIZATIONS

Alliance of Canadian Travel Associations (ACTA)
2560 Matheson Boulevard E., Suite 226
Mississauga, ON L4W 4Y9
Canada
(905) 282-9294
Website: http://www.acta.ca
Association of Canadian Travel Agencies (ACTA) is a
   national trade association representing the retail
   travel sector of Canada's tourism industry.

The Travel Institute
945 Concord Street
Framingham, MA 01701
(800) 542-4282
Website: http://www.thetravelinstitute.com
Through innovative education programs, professional
   certifications, and customized learning solutions,
   The Travel Institute fulfills its nonprofit mission
   to promote a standard of industry knowledge
   and excellence.

BOOKS

Ogg, Tom, and Joanie Ogg. *How to Start a Home Based Travel Agency*. Valley Center, CA: Tom Ogg & Associates, 2013.
Start Your Own Travel Business: Cruises, Adventure Travel, Tours, Senior Travel. Irvine, CA: Entrepreneur Press, 2012.

WEBSITES

Because of the changing nature of internet links, Rosen Publishing has developed an online list of websites related to the subject of this book. This site is updated regularly. Please use this link to access the list:

http://www.rosenlinks.com/CCWC/planning

CHAPTER 13

IMPORT/EXPORT COORDINATOR

Goods manufactured in the US for export to other countries and goods manufactured in other countries for import to the US require someone to handle the business of trade. Overseeing these transactions, from cars to sneakers, are shipping specialists or import/export coodinators.

WHAT THEY DO

Import is a big business, often filled with risks and is a trillion dollar industry. Exporting is just as big. In September 2016 alone, American companies exported $189.2 billion worth of goods to foreign countries, per the Bureau of Economic Analysis.

According to the US Census Bureau, the top ten countries with which the United States traded in 2016 were Canada, Mexico, Japan, China, Germany, the United Kingdom, France, South Korea, India, and Taiwan.

What sorts of things are imported or exported? Exports and imports may include raw materials, agricultural products, or manufactured goods, as well as services such as

Import and export of goods makes goods not manufactured or grown in a certain country available for sale in that country.

travel, banking, or telecommunications. All goods need to be carefully handled heading into or out of the United States.

Export managers direct foreign sales, negotiate sales and distribution contracts, and arrange payment between the manufacturer and retail sales outlet.

Custom brokers are the intermediaries between import/export specialists and customs agents in each country. They prepare the entry papers, file documents to allow delivery of goods, and assess duties and taxes that may be charged by any given country and must be licensed by the United States Department of the Treasury. "For every shipment entering the United States," according to the American Association of Exporters and

Importers (AAEI), "there are 500 pages of Customs regulations and thousands of tariff items. The broker must be well versed in determining proper classifications and dutiable value and be fully aware of the vast number of commodities subject to quotas. Customs brokers facilitate release of imported goods, pay required duties, and provide and maintain required records and documents. They may also help clients choose modes of transportation and specific carriers."

Freight forwarders are the agents, licensed by the Federal Maritime Commission or the International Air Transportation Association, for exporters to move cargo overseas. These people need to be familiar with import rules and regulations for each country, have a good working knowledge of United States export regulations, and be familiar with all methods of shipping appropriate to the goods, as well as special packaging needs or handling restrictions. The AAEI says, "Forwarders must be aware of regulations that affect cargo movements, such as hazardous materials rules, special handling or packing restrictions, licensing provisions, and foreign documentation requirements. Forwarders may coordinate arrangements for storage, full-container shipments and inland transportation."

PREPARING FOR YOUR CAREER

If you decide to become an export coordinator, there are several areas of expertise required. In all cases, training is available

COMMONLY USED IMPORT/EXPERT TERMS

Duties and tariffs are taxes levied by the government on the import, export, or use of goods. They are generally based on the value of the goods, some other factor, such as weight or quantity (specific duties), or a combination of value and other factors (compound duties). Governments may impose tariffs to protect particular domestic industries from imported goods or to raise revenue.

Harmonized Tariff Code Schedule is a system for classifying goods in international trade. More than fifty countries use the codes, which were introduced in 1989. The United States International Trade Commission's Office of Tariff Affairs and Trade Agreements is responsible for publishing the annotated Harmonized Tariff Schedule of the United States.

Trade compliance means countries abide by active, binding agreements with their trading partners covering imports and exports of goods and services. These countries are expected to comply with the terms of these agreements.

Trade security refers to the safety of international shipments of goods and the ability to keep these shipments free of penetration by terrorists or others with illegal intentions.

either through the employee or specialized schools that can help get you the required licensing. Attributes required for these positions are clear communication skills, good writing skills, and a familiarity with a second or third language.

Most of what is imported to a country is sent overseas in large shipping containers. People must keep highly accurate records to make sure that nothing goes amiss.

JOB OUTLOOK AND SALARY

A broker is usually paid according to what his or her trade is worth. Business operations specialists, per the Bureau of Labor Statistics, earn around $73,480 annually, on average. Experienced specialists can earn up to $116,000 per year.

One thing all the jobs have in common is that their job stability and growth are entirely dependent on global economic conditions that can change daily. Still, as the global economy continues to expand, leaving no country and continent unaffected, people will be required to know how to move goods and materials from one port to the next.

FOR MORE INFORMATION

ORGANIZATIONS

American Association of Exporters and Importers (AAEI)
1050 17th Street NW
Washington, DC 20036
(202) 857-8009
Website: http://www.aaei.org
AAEI is the premier trade organization representing US
companies engaged in global trade.

Canadian International Freight Forwarders Association
1243 Islington Avenue, Suite 706
Toronto, ON M8X 1Y9
Canada
(416) 234-5100
Website: http://www.ciffa.com
This association represents and supports members
of the Canadian international freight forwarding
industry in providing the highest level of quality and
professional services to their clients.

The National Customs Brokers & Forwarders Association
of America (NCBFAA)
1200 18th Street NW, #901

Washington, DC 20036
(202) 466-0222
Website: http://www.NCBFAA.org
The NCBFAA represents more than 970 member
companies with 110,000 employees in international
trade, the nation's leading freight forwarders, customs
brokers, ocean transportation intermediaries (OTIs),
and air cargo agents.

BOOKS

Start Your Own Import/Export Business: Your Step-by-Step Guide to Success. Irvine, CA: Entrepreneur Press, 2017.

WEBSITES

Because of the changing nature of internet links, Rosen Publishing has developed an online list of websites related to the subject of this book. This site is updated regularly. Please use this link to access the list:

http://www.rosenlinks.com/CCWC/planning

GLOSSARY

CHARITY An organization whose sole purpose is raising money for a particular cause.

CLIENT An individual or business with which someone has a professional relationship.

CONFIDENTIAL Something secret, often because release of materials might affect a professional relationship.

MULTITASKING The ability to handle a variety of tasks at once.

MUNDANE Uninteresting, boring, or repetitive.

PLANOGRAM A diagram that indicates placement of items on a store shelf to help with sales.

PRIVATE SECTOR Parts of the economy that are owned or controlled by private businesses or individuals.

PUBLIC SECTOR Parts of the economy that are owned and controlled by the government.

RÉSUMÉ A list of professional accomplishments, intended to show potential employers one's job qualifications.

TARIFF A government tax on imported or exported goods.

BIBLIOGRAPHY

Beckman, Kate. "11 Things I Wish I Knew Before I Became a Personal Assistant." *Cosmopolitan*, January 8, 2016. http://www.cosmopolitan.com/career/a50766/things-i-wish-i-knew-before-i-became-a-personal-assistant.

Cunningham, Katelan. "How to Quit Your Job and Become a Professional Organizer." BRIT+CO, May 19, 2015. http://www.brit.co/how-to-get-into-professional-organizing.

Davis, Noah. "How Do You Make a Living, Auctioneer?" *Pacific Standard*, January 14, 2015. https://psmag.com/how-do-you-make-a-living-auctioneer-8e4d919e276d#.dod8cjapw.

Garecht, Joe. "How Anyone Can Be a Superstar Fundraiser." The Fundraising Authority. Retrieved December 6, 2016. http://www.thefundraisingauthority.com/fundraising-basics/be-a-superstar-fundraiser.

McKay, Dawn Rosenberg. "Here Comes the...Wedding Planner." The Balance, October 12, 2016. https://www.thebalance.com/here-comes-the-wedding-planner-525966.

The U.S. Bureau of Labor Statistics. Retrieved April 24, 2017. https://www.bls.gov.

INDEX

ABOUT THE AUTHOR

Rebecca Pelos is a nonfiction writer with experience in job hunting and career guidance. She lives in Tennessee.

Robert Greenberger has been organizing things all his life, starting with a series of jobs at his high school and college newspaper. At DC Comics, he was manager of editorial operations, and at Marvel Comics he was director of publishing operations. A graduate of SUNY-Binghamton, he currently is a senior editor at DC Comics and also does a lot of freelance writing requiring a careful balance between work, freelance, and home obligations. He makes his home in Connecticut with his wife, Deb, and children, Kate and Robbie.

PHOTO CREDITS

Cover, p. 1 Dynamic Graphics/Creatas/Thinkstock; p. 5 Antonio Guillem/Shutterstock.com; p. 7 oliveromg/Shutterstock.com; p. 11 freya-photographer/Shutterstock.com; p. 16 © iStockphoto.com/Christopher Futcher; p. 18 Uber Images/Shutterstock.com; p. 24 Christopher Robbins/Photodisc/Thinkstock; p. 30 leungchopan/Shutterstock.com; p. 35 © iStockphoto.com/trekandshoot; p. 38 © iStockphoto.com/Weekend Images Inc.; p. 44 Julie Dermansky/Corbis News/Getty Images; p. 47 steve bridge/Shutterstock.com; p. 56 Bloomberg/Getty Images; p. 59 © iStockphoto.com/Yuri Arcurs; p. 65 Dragon Images/Shutterstock.com; p. 68 michaeljung/Shutterstock.com; p. 75 © iStockphoto.com/vgajic; p. 78 © iStockphoto.com/monkeybusinessimages; p. 86 © iStockphoto.com/Jen Grantham; p. 89 mark peterson/Corbis Historical/Getty Images; p. 94 Alain Le Garsmeur/Hulton Archive/Getty Images; p. 99 aerogondo2/Shutterstock.com; p. 103 Aila Images/Shutterstock.com; p. 105 ESB Essentials/Shutterstock.com; p. 110 Pressmaster/Shutterstock.com; p. 112 ESB Professional/Shutterstock.com; p. 118 T photography/Shutterstock.com; p. 121 Shestakoff/Shutterstock.com; cover and interior design elements © iStockphoto.com/David Shultz (dots), Melamory/Shutterstock.com (hexagon pattern), Lost & Taken (boxed text background texture), bioraven/Shutterstock.com (chapter opener pages icons).

Designer: Brian Garvey; Editor and Photo Researcher: Bethany Bryan